THE SAND TIGER SHARK

By Megan Borgert-Spaniol

BELLWETHER MEDIA · MINNEAPOLIS, MN

Jump into the cockpit and take flight with Pilot books. Your journey will take you on high-energy adventures as you learn about all that is wild, weird, fascinating, and fun!

This edition first published in 2013 by Bellwether Media, Inc.

No part of this publication may be reproduced in whole or in part without written permission of the publisher. For information regarding permission, write to Bellwether Media, Inc., Attention: Permissions Department, 5357 Penn Avenue South, Minneapolis, MN 55419.

Library of Congress Cataloging-in-Publication Data

Borgert-Spaniol, Megan, 1989-
  The sand tiger shark / by Megan Borgert-Spaniol.
     p. cm. – (Pilot books : shark fact files)
  Includes bibliographical references and index.
  Summary: "Engaging images accompany information about the sand tiger shark. The combination of high-interest subject matter and narrative text is intended for students in grades 3 through 7"–Provided by publisher.
  ISBN 978-1-60014-806-4 (hardcover : alk. paper)
  1. Sand tiger shark–Juvenile literature. I. Title.
  QL638.95.O3B67 2013
  597.3'3–dc23
                       2012002605

Printed in the United States of America, North Mankato, MN.

TABLE OF CONTENTS

Sand Tiger Shark: **Identified** 4

Sand Tiger Shark: **Tracked** 10

Sand Tiger Shark: **Current Status** ...16

Glossary 22

To Learn More 23

Index.. 24

SAND TIGER SHARK
IDENTIFIED

A dive crew descends on the wreck of the *Dixie Arrow* off the coast of Cape Hatteras. German forces sunk this American ship in 1942. Now it rests at a depth of 90 feet (27 meters). It is one of the most popular dive sites in North Carolina.

As the crew approaches the shipwreck, they see the long shadows of sand tiger sharks. The sharks remain still as schools of tiny fish hurry past. A diver swims closer to one of the sharks and comes face-to-face with a mouthful of razor-sharp teeth. The sand tiger shark does not attack. Instead, it

Sand tiger sharks inhabit warm coastal waters in every ocean except the eastern Pacific. They are named after their sandy homes along the ocean floor of the **surf zone**. Sand tiger sharks often return to the same spot every year to mate. Shipwrecks and **coral reefs** are popular meeting points. Gatherings of up to 80 sand tiger sharks are common around shipwrecks off the east coast of the United States.

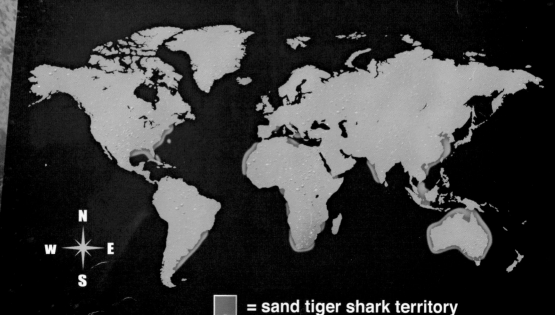

= sand tiger shark territory

The sand tiger shark is not aggressive, but it has a threatening look. It often swims with its mouth open. Rows of long, ragged teeth stick out in every direction. Behind the jaws is a bulky body. It can measure up to 10.5 feet (3.2 meters) and weigh up to 350 pounds (159 kilograms). The sand tiger shark uses eight fins to move. A large **caudal fin** propels the shark forward. The other fins help it turn, stop, and stay upright.

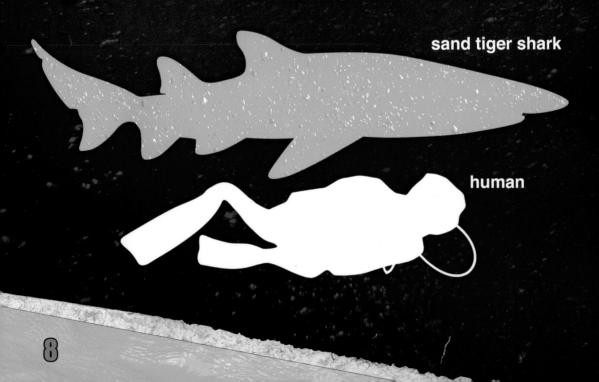

sand tiger shark

human

Sand tiger sharks shed most of their teeth over two-week periods. New teeth move forward from back rows to replace the old ones.

Sand tiger sharks are **ovoviviparous**. This means they develop in eggs within the **uterus**. A female sand tiger shark has two uteruses. Each uterus holds many eggs. The largest pups that hatch eat the smaller pups and unhatched eggs. After 8 to 12 months, the mother gives birth to two grown pups. The newborns are 3 feet (1 meter) long and weigh around 13 pounds (6 kilograms). They can swim and eat on their own.

A young sand tiger shark can be prey for larger sharks. Its **countershading** helps it blend in with its surroundings. Rust-colored spots on the shark's back look like the sandy ocean floor. The spots fade as the shark grows and other predators become less of a threat.

young sand tiger shark

MOSSY JAWS

Researchers believe that female sand tiger sharks stop feeding for several weeks while they are pregnant. Moss grows on their teeth while they are not in use.

During the day, sand tiger sharks stay around underwater caves and cliffs. At night they sweep the ocean floor in search of prey. They are the only sharks known to float motionless in the water. To do this, they swim to the surface and swallow air. This makes them **buoyant**. The sharks can then sink by letting air out.

The needle-like teeth of a sand tiger shark are best suited for small prey that can be swallowed whole. Some of the shark's favorite fish are snapper, sea bass, flounder, and eel. It will sometimes feast on crabs, lobsters, and squid. Every so often it will go after smaller sharks.

The sand tiger shark uses sensors to guide it to prey. The **ampullae of Lorenzini** lie beneath the surface of a shark's skin. They detect the weak **electric fields** of nearby prey. The sand tiger shark also depends on its nose to find food. It can sniff out a meal from miles away!

A TEAM EFFORT

Sand tiger sharks sometimes hunt in groups. They surround schools of fish and force them together. This makes the fish easier to catch.

SAND TIGER SHARK

CURRENT STATUS

In the 1950s and 1960s, it was common for divers in Australia to kill sand tiger sharks. Some thought the sharks were dangerous and acted in self-defense. Others knew the sharks were not a threat. They killed for the thrill alone. The numbers lost during this time have greatly reduced the sand tiger shark population.

Sand tiger sharks are still caught for food in the North Pacific and Indian Oceans. They are also hunted off the west coast of Africa. Their meat is especially popular in Japan. It is sold fresh, frozen, smoked, and dried. The liver is taken for its oil, and the skin is used for leather. The shark fin trade puts a high price on dried fins. They are used in shark fin soup. Even the jaws and teeth of the sand tiger shark are seen as trophies.

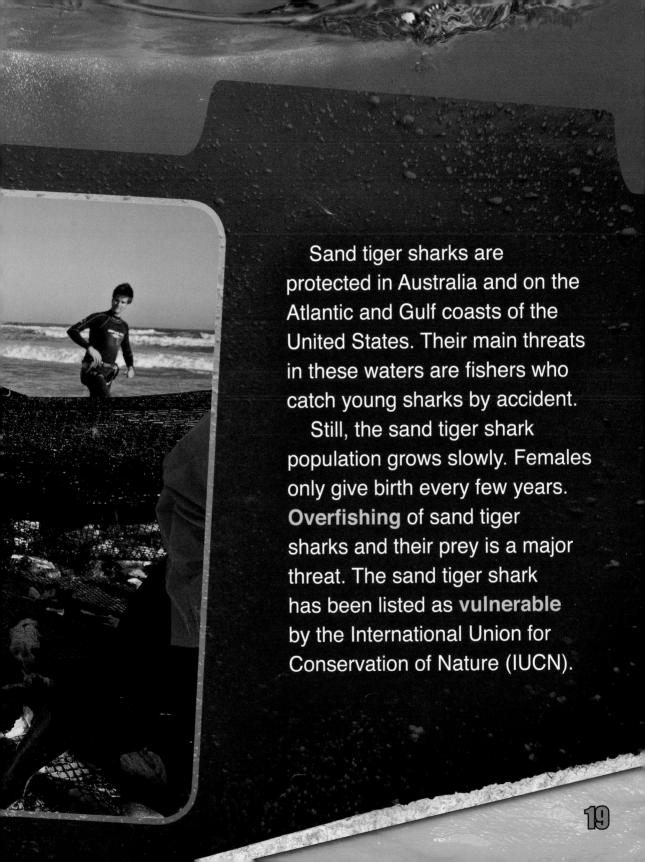

Sand tiger sharks are protected in Australia and on the Atlantic and Gulf coasts of the United States. Their main threats in these waters are fishers who catch young sharks by accident.

Still, the sand tiger shark population grows slowly. Females only give birth every few years. **Overfishing** of sand tiger sharks and their prey is a major threat. The sand tiger shark has been listed as **vulnerable** by the International Union for Conservation of Nature (IUCN).

SHARK BRIEF

Common Name: Sand Tiger Shark

Also Known As: Grey Nurse Shark
Spotted Ragged-Tooth Shark
Sand Shark

Claim to Fame: Long, ragged teeth

Hot Spots: Eastern United States
Gulf of Mexico
Southeastern South America
Southern Europe
Mediterranean Sea
South Africa
Australia
Eastern Asia
Red Sea

Life Span: 15 years or more

Current Status: Vulnerable (IUCN)

EXTINCT

EXTINCT IN THE WILD

CRITICALLY ENDANGERED

ENDANGERED

VULNERABLE

NEAR THREATENED

LEAST CONCERN

It is very rare for a sand tiger shark to attack a human. Most attacks occur in murky waters. The shark mistakes a swimmer's hand or foot for a small fish. It is usually quick to let go. However, even a brief encounter with its ragged

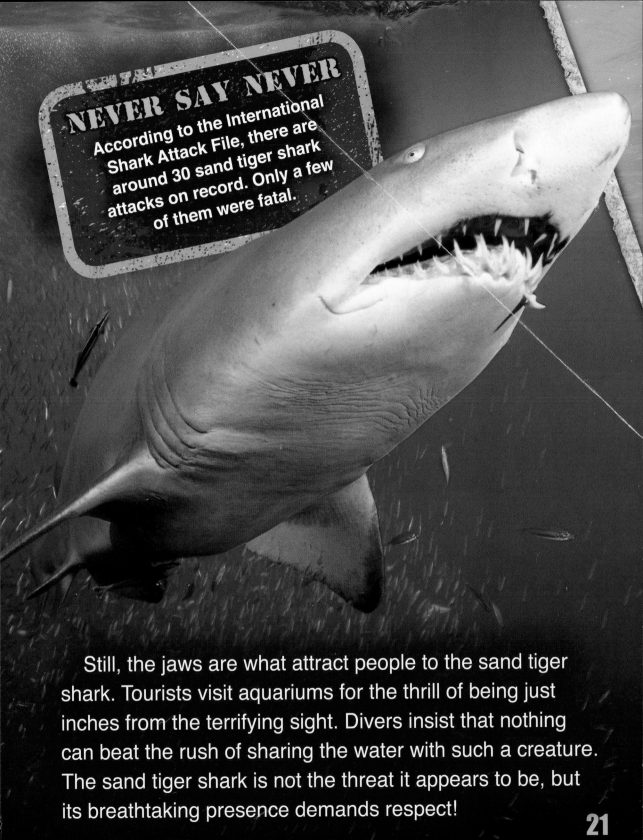

Still, the jaws are what attract people to the sand tiger shark. Tourists visit aquariums for the thrill of being just inches from the terrifying sight. Divers insist that nothing can beat the rush of sharing the water with such a creature. The sand tiger shark is not the threat it appears to be, but its breathtaking presence demands respect!

GLOSSARY

ampullae of Lorenzini—a network of tiny jelly-filled sacs around a shark's snout; the jelly is sensitive to the electric fields of nearby prey.

buoyant—able to float

caudal fin—the tail fin of a fish; the sand tiger shark's caudal fin has two lobes, or sections.

coral reefs—underwater structures off coasts; coral reefs are made of the skeletons of animals called corals.

countershading—coloring that helps camouflage an animal; fish with countershading have pale bellies and dark backs.

electric fields—waves of electricity created by movement; every living being has an electric field.

overfishing—greatly reducing the number of fish in an area by fishing too much

ovoviviparous—producing young that develop in eggs inside the body; ovoviviparous animals give birth to live young.

surf zone—the area where waves form and break near shore

uterus—a protective chamber inside some female animals; sand tiger sharks develop in eggs inside either of the mother's two uteruses.

vulnerable—at risk of becoming endangered

TO LEARN MORE

At the Library

Burnham, Brad. *The Sand Tiger Shark*. New York, N.Y.: PowerKids Press, 2001.

Llewellyn, Claire. *The Best Book of Sharks*. New York, N.Y.: Kingfisher, 1999.

Musgrave, Ruth. *National Geographic Kids Everything Sharks*. Washington, D.C.: National Geographic, 2011.

On the Web

Learning more about sand tiger sharks is as easy as 1, 2, 3.

1. Go to www.factsurfer.com.

2. Enter "sand tiger sharks" into the search box.

3. Click the "Surf" button and you will see a list of related Web sites.

With factsurfer.com, finding more information is just a click away.

INDEX

Africa, 16
attacks, 20, 21
Australia, 16, 19
Cape Hatteras, 4
coral reefs, 7
countershading, 10
divers, 4, 16, 21
eggs, 10
fins, 8, 16
hot spots, 20
International Union for
    Conservation of Nature
    (IUCN), 19, 20
Japan, 16
jaws, 8, 16, 21
life span, 20
North Carolina, 4
overfishing, 19
population, 16, 19
predators, 10

prey, 13, 14, 15, 19
pups, 10
reproduction, 10, 11, 19
senses, 15
shipwrecks, 4, 7
size, 8, 10
surf zone, 7
teeth, 4, 8, 9, 11, 14, 16, 20
territory, 7
threats, 16, 19
United States, 7, 19